THINGS I SCREAM IN MY HEAD AT WORK

HOW TO SURVIVE A TOXIC WORKPLACE WITHOUT LOSING YOUR MIND

AMELIA OLIVER-LILLY

THINGS I SCREAM IN MY HEAD AT WORK

First edition
Paperback and eBook

Cover and interior design by Big Fat Web
Published by Upload Makers Publishing

CONTENTS

CHAPTER 3

MEETINGS, EMAILS AND OTHER DAILY TORTURE DEVICES

CHAPTER 4

COWORKERS: LEGENDS, NIGHTMARES AND WALKING RED FLAGS

CHAPTER 7
MAKING WORK SLIGHTLY LESS AWFUL

8

INTRODUCTION

SO, YOUR JOB IS RIDICULOUS.

THIS BOOK IS FOR THE THOUGHTS YOU DON'T SAY OUT LOUD.

There's a reason you're reading a book called *Things I Scream In My Head At Work*, and it's not because everything at your job is fine.

Maybe your boss is a human fire alarm. Maybe every "quick meeting" steals an hour of your life. Maybe you spend most days smiling politely while your inner voice runs full commentary in all caps.

Out loud, you say things like:

- *"Sounds good."*
- *"No worries."*
- *"Happy to help."*

Inside your head, you're thinking:

- "This is insane!"
- "Why am I the only one who sees this is a bad idea?"
- "Are you f*cking kidding me?"

This book lives in that gap. The space between your **outside voice** that wants to stay employed and your **inside voice** that would very much like to flip a table.

You're not lazy. You're not weak. You're not "too sensitive for the real world."

You're a reasonably decent human stuck in a **toxic workplace**, surrounded by other humans, some of them great and some of them absolute idiots.

You care about getting paid, you care about not losing your mind, and you're tired of pretending everything's fine when it clearly isn't.

If you take nothing else from this book, take this: **don't live to work, work to live**. Your job is supposed to fund your life, not become your entire personality.

Work is one part of your world. It's not the whole story, and it sure as hell is not the most important character.

This book isn't here to:

- teach you to "love" your company
- help you manifest your dream job with positive vibes
- turn you into the perfect corporate robot

I'm not your CEO, I'm not HR, and I'm not your mindfulness app or coach.

But, I'm on your side.

What this book's actually about

This is a **survival guide for your inner voice**.

It's for people who:

- can't just quit tomorrow
- still need the paycheck
- are slowly being cooked by a toxic workplace
- want to stay sane without turning into a full-time doormat

You're not getting a neat seven step leadership model or inspirational quotes from billionaires. You're getting things like:

- scripts for what to say out loud when your brain's yelling "are you f*cking kidding me"
- ways to protect your time and energy when everyone treats you like an endless resource
- ways to deal with bad bosses, dramatic coworkers, and pointless meetings without losing your mind
- tiny acts of rebellion that remind you you're still a person, not just an employee ID
- practical steps to figure out whether you're staying for now or quietly planning your escape

You're allowed to laugh at how ridiculous it all is. You're also allowed to admit that sometimes it genuinely hurts. Both can live in the same book.

How to use this thing without turning it into homework

You don't have to read this cover to cover like a training manual. Dip in where it stings.

- If you feel trapped between what you **want** to say and what you **actually** say, start around the communication and "things I wish I could say" chapter.
- If meetings and email are your personal hell, go straight to the chapters about daily torture devices.
- If coworkers and managers are your main headache, jump into the people chapters.
- If you're already thinking about leaving, skip ahead to the exit plan.

Each chapter's built to:

- make you feel seen,
- let you smirk instead of only rage, and
- give you one or two concrete things you can try in real life.

This isn't a perfect system you have to implement. It's a toolbox. Take what helps, ignore what doesn't, come back whenever your job pulls another stunt.

About the swearing, the jokes and the serious bits

You're going to see words like **bullshit**, **idiots**, **shitshow** and **f*ck** in this book. They're aimed at systems and behavior, not at you and not at vulnerable groups.

If that bothers you more than unpaid overtime, you've probably bought the wrong book. That's fine. There are plenty of polite corporate titles out there.

Also, this matters:

This book's **not** medical, legal, HR or psychological advice. It's not a replacement for therapy, a doctor or a lawyer. It's one fed up human talking to another about how to stay sane in a work environment that often feels like a circus.

If your job's pushed you to the point where you're:

- not sleeping
- crying regularly
- feeling numb most of the time
- fantasizing about getting mildly injured so you don't have to go in

then please talk to a doctor, therapist or other qualified professional. Use this book alongside that, not instead of it. Your brain and body matter more than any job.

QUICK NOTE: this book isn't here to claim every workplace is a shithole. Some people have genuinely good teams, fair managers, and days that don't feel like survival training. If that's you, congratulations, please stay there.

This book is for everyone else, the ones white-knuckling through chaos, nonsense, and "urgent" requests that magically appear five minutes before you log off.

You're NOT the problem

Toxic workplaces are great at making you feel like you're the issue.

- You're not organized enough.
- You're not resilient enough.
- You're not committed enough.

Funny how the solution's always "you personally should do more" and never "maybe this place is run like a dumpster fire."

The thread running through every chapter is this:

- You're not crazy for thinking your workplaces is ridiculous.
- You're not a failure for struggling in a badly run system.
- You didn't hire your boss.
- You didn't design the processes.
- You didn't choose the culture.

You're just trying to survive it without becoming a hollow shell who only feels alive on Friday nights.

What you can expect by the end
By the time you finish this book, I hope you'll:

- stop gaslighting yourself about how bad things actually are
- have better words to use out loud when your inner voice's screaming
- feel less alone and a bit more in on the joke
- know whether you're staying for now or plotting your escape
- remember you're a whole person with a life beyond this job

You'll still have rough days. Some meetings will still be stupid. Some people will still be idiots. That's the honest reality of a toxic workplace.

The difference is you'll have more tools, more language and more perspective. You'll know how to protect yourself a little better. You'll know that staying's a **choice**, not a life sentence.

Your mouth can keep saying "sounds good" when it has to.

Your brain can keep yelling "are you f*cking kidding me" in private.

And somewhere between the two, you can build a version of working life where you keep your paycheck, your sanity and at least part of your sense of humor.

Remember: *Don't live to work. Work to live.*

Let's get into it.

CHAPTER 1
IT'S NOT JUST YOU

There's a difference between a job that's occasionally annoying and a job that slowly eats your brain. You already know which one you've got.

You drag yourself into another day, open your inbox, stare at your calendar and think some version of:

- "How is this my life?"

- "Why is everything urgent and nothing makes sense?"

- "If one more person says 'quick question,' I'm putting myself on 'Do Not Disturb' permanently."

On the outside you look "fine". You show up. You hit deadlines. You smile in meetings. You say *"sounds good"* when your boss drops a last-minute task on a Friday afternoon.

Inside, it's a different show.

That's where **things you scream in your head at work** actually live.

Common symptoms that your job has crossed the line into toxic territory:

- You feel dread in your chest on Sunday afternoon, not just a mild "ugh, Monday."

- You're tired all the time, even when you're not doing anything physically demanding.

- You re-run conversations in your head at night, imagining what you wish you'd said.

- You fantasize about quitting on the spot, then immediately panic because you need the money.

None of that means you're broken. It means your workplace is heavy, and your nervous system's yelling, "Hey, something's off here."

[1.2] TOXIC WORKPLACES MESS WITH YOUR HEAD

Toxic workplaces don't always look like screaming bosses and public humiliation. Some do. Most are sneakier than that.

They mess with you in quieter ways:

- Expectations keep changing and somehow, it's always your fault.
- You're constantly told to "own it" but given almost no actual control.
- You're praised for pushing through ridiculous workloads, then expected to keep doing it forever.
- You're told "we're a family" right before they ask for unpaid extra effort.

After a while, you start doubting your own reality.

You think:

- "Maybe I'm just not tough enough."
- "Maybe everyone else is fine with this and I'm the weird one."
- "Maybe this is just what being an adult is."

Spoiler: it's not "just being an adult" to grind your mental health into the floor for the sake of someone else's targets.

Toxic workplaces rely on you thinking **you're** the problem so you keep trying harder instead of asking whether the whole setup is cooked.

[1.3] THE STORIES YOU TELL YOURSELF TO SURVIVE

Most people in bad jobs end up telling themselves little stories so they can get through the day. You might recognize a few.

Story 1: "It's just a busy season."
You've been saying this for 18 months. The season is now your whole climate. There is no "after." This is it.

Story 2: "Once this project is over, it'll calm down."
The project ends. Two more appear. Someone leaves. You inherit half their work "for a bit." It never really calms down.

Story 3: "Everyone else is coping better than me."
They're not. They're just better at faking it, or they've numbed out so hard they don't feel anything anymore.

Story 4: "I'm lucky to have a job at all."
You can be grateful for income and still admit the way you're treated is crap. Those two truths can sit next to each other.

These stories make it feel slightly less awful in the moment. The problem is they all quietly say the same thing:

"The situation can't change, so I have to."

Sometimes that's true in the short term. You can't magically swap jobs tomorrow. But if you keep swallowing the idea that the only option is "try harder and shut up," you burn out while the system stays exactly the same.

[1.4] WHY YOU BLAME YOURSELF (AND WHY THAT'S WRONG)

It's strangely easier to believe **you're** the issue than to accept that your whole environment is messed up.

If you're the problem, you can fix it. Work harder. Be more organized. Toughen up. Say yes to everything and maybe one day someone will reward you.

If the system's the problem, that's scarier. It means:

- No matter how perfect you are, it'll still be chaotic.
- No matter how much you give, it'll never feel like enough.
- No matter how hard you try, you can't control what people above you choose to do.

So, you blame yourself because it feels like the only place you have any control.

The truth sits in the middle:

- Yes, you have some responsibility for your choices.
- No, you didn't create this circus.
- No, you're not required to destroy your health to prove you're "a team player."

You're allowed to look at your workplace and say, "This setup is stupid," without adding, "and that's my personal moral failure."

[1.5] WHAT YOU'RE ACTUALLY ALLOWED TO WANT FROM WORK

Let's be clear about something workplaces rarely say out loud.

You're allowed to want:

- A paycheck that covers more than just survival.
- Work that doesn't constantly make you feel like an idiot.
- A manager who treats you like a human, not a resource.
- Reasonable hours most of the time.
- To log off and have a life that doesn't revolve around your inbox.

You're also allowed to want **respect**. This does not mean endless praise and balloons. It means:

- People listen when you say there's a problem.
- You're not routinely thrown under the bus to protect someone else.
- Your time isn't treated like an infinite free buffet.

Wanting these things doesn't make you entitled. It makes you awake.

Toxic workplaces love to label basic needs as "unrealistic." They'll tell you "this is just how it is" so you feel silly for hoping for anything better.

Hold on to this:

Wanting to stay sane and be treated decently in a job is not asking for too much.

[1.6] YOU'RE NOT ALONE IN YOUR INNER SCREAMING

One of the clever tricks of a toxic workplace is isolation. Everyone's stressed. Everyone's overloaded. Nobody has energy left to compare notes.

So, you sit at your desk thinking:

- "Is it just me who thinks this is insane?"

- "Am I the only one who feels completely fried?"

- "Maybe I'm overreacting and everyone else is fine?"

Newsflash: you're absolutely not the only one.

Other people are:

- smiling on camera in meetings while silently counting down the minutes

- typing "thanks!" in chat while thinking "what is this bullshit"

- nodding along in "vision" sessions while quietly opening job boards in another tab

You might not hear their exact **things they scream in their head at work**, but they're there.

This book exists partly so you can read a line and think, "Oh. It's not just me. Someone else has seen this too."

[1.7] HOW THIS CHAPTER FITS INTO THE BIGGER PICTURE

This first chapter's job is simple:

- *Tell yourself* you're not crazy.
- *Tell yourself* you're not alone.
- *Tell yourself* your job might actually be the problem, not your entire personality.

From here, we're going to get more specific:

- The next chapter digs into the gap between what you **want** to say and what you **actually** say, and gives you ways to handle that without getting fired.
- Later chapters zoom in on meetings, email, coworkers, managers, HR, boundaries and your eventual escape plan.

But none of that matters if you secretly believe you're just weak and everyone else is thriving. You'll read the advice and quietly think, "Yeah, but that's for people who deserve better. I'm just bad at coping."

So, let's nail this now:

- *You're not* overreacting because you're tired of being treated like an endless resource.
- *You're not* dramatic because your brain's yelling "are you f*cking kidding me" every second day.
- *You're not* failing at adulthood because this job feels like too much.

You're a normal human reacting normally to a pretty messed up environment.

[1.8] A SMALL REFRAME TO TAKE WITH YOU

Before you move on, try one small mental shift.

Instead of thinking:
"I'm terrible at my job."
try:
"I'm doing my job inside a system that makes everything harder than it needs to be."

Instead of:
"I can't handle work like other people can."
try:
"This setup would exhaust a lot of people. My reactions make sense."

Instead of:
"I shouldn't feel this angry and checked out."
try:
"My anger is a signal that something isn't okay here."

Your inner voice doesn't make you weak. It's the part of you that still cares enough to notice something's wrong.

Try this:
Over the next week, when you catch your brain screaming at work, don't shut it down. Mentally label it: "Oh look, another thing I scream in my head at work." You don't have to act on it yet. Just notice how often it happens. That's not you being dramatic. That's data.

In the next chapter, we'll start turning those internal rants into actual words you can use out loud without blowing up your career.

Chapter 2
Shit You Want To Say vs What You Actually Say

[2.1] The gap between your brain and your mouth

Your brain at work:
- "Are you serious right now"
- "This is a terrible idea."
- "Do you actually hear yourself speak."

Your mouth at work:
- *"Sure, sounds good."*
- *"Yep, I can look into that."*
- *"Thanks for the update."*

Welcome to the gap.

This chapter lives right in the space between **what you want to say** and **what you actually say** so you can keep your job, your sanity and your future references.

You're not imagining it.

A lot of modern work is built on:

- pretending things are fine when they're not

- calling disasters "challenges"

- saying "no problem" while staring at a huge, very real problem

No one trained you for this. School didn't teach "How to say what you mean without getting dragged into HR." Your first job probably rewarded you for being nice and eager, not for setting boundaries.

So, you learned to swallow a lot of truth. You learned to translate "what the hell" into "no worries."

This chapter is about giving you **better translations**. Not fake ones. Honest ones that won't blow everything up.

[2.2] WHY YOU CAN'T JUST "SAY WHAT YOU THINK"

There's always someone who says, "I just tell it like it is."
That person is either:

- unemployed
- constantly in trouble
- or secretly backed by so much power that they can get away with it

For the rest of us, "saying what you think" word for word is a quick way to:

- burn bridges
- build enemies
- become *The Difficult One* people avoid

You're not wrong for wanting to speak your mind. You're just playing a game where the rules are stacked against blunt honesty.

Most workplaces don't reward "truth." They reward **comfort**. They reward people who make problems sound small, deliver bad news with a smile, and keep everyone feeling like they're still in control. "Just be honest" is usually advice from someone who won't be the one labeled "aggressive," "difficult," or "not a team player" the second the honesty lands wrong.

Also, blunt honesty rarely gets heard the way you mean it. It triggers ego, defensiveness, and office politics. The moment the other person feels attacked, you've lost the point and you're now in a side quest called "Explain Your Tone." Translation isn't you being fake. It's you getting the truth into the room **without becoming the problem for saying it.**

The trick is not to silence yourself. The trick is to **say the important part** in a way that:

- gets heard
- doesn't start World War Three
- let's you sleep at night because you didn't completely betray yourself

Think of it like subtitles.

Your brain runs the uncensored version:

"You've given me a two-day job with a one-hour deadline, you clown."

Your mouth offers the edited version:

"With the current workload, I can't do that by today without dropping something else. Which should we move."

Same reality. Different delivery. One might get you fired. One puts the problem back where it belongs.

[2.3] THE HONEST-BUT-FIRED VERSION VS THE HONEST-AND-EMPLOYED VERSION

Let's take some classic "shit I want to say" moments and run them through translation.

Scenario 1: The last minute "quick favor"

What your brain screams:
"You had this for a week, now it's my emergency? Get f*cked."

What your mouth usually says:
"Yeah, I can do that."

What you could say instead:
"I can help with part of this. Right now, I've got A, B and C on my plate. If this is now my top priority, what should I move to next week?"

You're not attacking; you're making the trade-off visible and asking them to choose.

Scenario 2: The pointless, meandering meeting

What your brain screams:
"We could've solved this with a three-line email."

What your mouth usually says:
Smiles, nods, adds nothing.

What you could say instead:
"To keep us on track, can we agree what we're deciding by the end of this meeting?"

Later, if it's always the same chaos, you can add:

"Could we try sending out an agenda beforehand so people can come ready with questions and decisions?"

Translated: "Stop wasting everyone's time," but in a way that a reasonable adult can't really argue with.

Scenario 3: The boss who changes direction every five minutes

What your brain screams:
"If you change your mind again, I'm going to start charging by the version."

What your mouth usually says:
"Okay, no problem, I'll redo it."

What you could say instead:
"Just so I'm clear, last week we agreed on X. Today you're saying Y. Is this the new direction, or are we still deciding?"

If they confirm the change:

"Thanks. For next time, it would really help if we locked the direction before I build the whole thing. That way I'm not redoing work and we save time."

You're calmly pointing out the cost of their chaos. You're not screaming, *"You're impossible,"* even if that's what your brain's yelling.

Scenario 4: The coworker who dumps their work on you

What your brain screams:
"I'm not your assistant, do your own job."

What your mouth usually says:
"Yeah, I can do that."

What you could say instead:
"I've got a full list already, so I can't take this on. If you're stuck on a specific part, I can help you think it through for a few minutes."

You're offering limited help without adopting their responsibilities as your own.

Scenario 5: The "can you just" from someone senior

What your brain screams:
"No, I can't 'just' do that. You've dropped a grenade and called it a paperclip."

What your mouth usually says:
"Sure, I'll sort it."

What you could say instead:
"I can start on that, yes. Given my current priorities, it'll likely be done by [realistic time]. If you need it sooner, we'll have to move [X] or [Y]."

Again, you're not flat out refusing. You're making the reality visible so they have to own the trade-off.

[2.4] THE "HR SAFE TRANSLATIONS" CHEAT SHEET

Your brain: "What the hell" … Your mouth: *can't say that.*

Here are some phrases you can use to translate rage into something that still tells the truth.

- **"I see it differently."**
  Translation: You're wrong, but I'm not starting a brawl about it.
- **"Can you walk me through the reasoning behind that decision?"**
  Translation: That sounds stupid, please explain yourself.
- **"I don't have capacity to take that on right now."**
  Translation: My plate's already overflowing, stop dumping more on it.
- **"What's the priority here?"**
  Translation: You've given me 10 urgent things. Pick one.
- **"Help me understand the timelines."**
  Translation: This deadline makes no sense.
- **"To be honest, that doesn't feel sustainable."**
  Translation: This is burning people out.
- **"That's outside my role, so I'd need clarity before I commit."**
  Translation: That's not my job.
- **"I'm not comfortable agreeing to that without [X]."**
  Translation: This is a bad idea and I'm not signing my name to it.

You don't need to sound like a robot. You're just giving your mouth a few more options than *"sure"* and *"no worries." Try this:* Pick one of these phrases and use it once this week. Just once. Notice how it feels to say it, and what happens when you do.

[2.5] SAYING NO WITHOUT STARTING A COLD WAR

"Just say no" is cute advice from people who don't have to live with the fallout.

You can say no. You just need to be strategic about how.

Good *no's* usually include:

- what you **can't** do
- what you **can** do
- the **reason** in simple terms

Example:

"I can't take on the whole report this time. I can contribute a section if the deadline stays Friday. Anything more will slip because of [X project]."

Or:

"I can't work late tonight; I've got plans I can't move. I can log on earlier tomorrow to finish my part."

You don't owe anyone your private life story. "Plans I can't move" covers kids, doctors, sleep, dinner with a friend, or you simply wanting to stare at a wall in peace.

You're not being difficult. You're refusing to be treated like a piece of software someone can run 24/7.

[2.6] WHEN YOU ACTUALLY SHOULD SAY THE BLUNT VERSION

Sometimes the "inside voice" version needs to be said out loud. Not word for word, but close enough that everyone gets the message.

You'll feel it when:

- something crosses an ethical line
- someone's safety is on the line
- someone's blaming you for something you didn't do
- you've tried the soft version ten times and nothing changes

In those moments, you're not just protecting your comfort. You're protecting yourself, your values or your job.

You can still be clear without blowing up. For example:

"I need to be really clear that this deadline was moved without my input, and I flagged the risk at the time. I'm not comfortable being held solely responsible for the delay."

Or:

"I'm not okay with how that was said in the meeting. It felt personal, not about the work. That can't happen again."

Your brain might be screaming, "You humiliated me, screw you."

Your mouth says, *"I'm not okay with that, and here's the line."* That's not drama. That's self-respect.

[2.7] WHAT NOT TO PUT IN WRITING (EVEN IF IT FEELS GOOD)

Quick reality check: your emails and DMs are **receipts**. Before you hit send on anything spicy, remember:

- screenshots exist
- "private" channels aren't really private
- tone is easy to misread in text

Stuff that's usually safer **out loud** or in your notes app instead of in writing:

- calling someone an idiot
- accusing someone of bad intent
- any sentence you'd be terrified to see on a big projector in a meeting

If you need to document something serious, stick to:

- what happened
- when it happened
- who was there
- how it affected the work

Example: "In yesterday's 3pm meeting, you raised your voice and said X. I felt uncomfortable being spoken to like that in front of the team. I want us to address concerns about my work without it getting personal."

Dry facts. Clear impact. No swear words.

You can still text your friend later and say, "My boss was an absolute deadshit." Just don't send that to the boss by accident.

[2.8] GIVING YOURSELF PERMISSION TO NOT BE "NICE" ALL THE TIME

If you've spent years being the "nice one," this chapter might make you slightly itchy.

You might be thinking:

- "I don't want to be rude."
- "I don't want to cause drama."
- "I don't want people to dislike me."

Here's the quiet truth:

- People will use you as much as you let them.
- Being endlessly "nice" reads as "available for more work."
- You can be kind and still say no.

Kindness is:

- giving people clarity
- not badmouthing them behind their back all day
- doing what you said you'd do

Self-betrayal is:

- saying yes when you're screaming no inside
- taking the hit for other people's laziness
- smiling through behavior that's not okay

You're not here to win "nicest doormat" of the year.

You're here to get your work done, protect your sanity, and leave with your self-respect intact.

Being "nice" is often just a polite costume you learned to wear so things don't get awkward. But in a toxic workplace, "nice" gets translated as "safe target" or "easy yes." You don't need to become rude. You just need to stop being automatically agreeable. There is a big difference between being kind and being convenient.

Also, let's be honest, the moment you stop being the easy one, people might act weird about it. That doesn't mean you did anything wrong. It means they were benefiting from the old version of you. Boundaries feel like drama to people who were enjoying your silence. Let them be uncomfortable. You've been uncomfortable for ages.

Think of it like this: you're not "being mean," you're being clear. Clear sounds like: "I can't take that on." "I'm at capacity." "No, that doesn't work for me." And when they push (because they will), you don't explain yourself into a puddle. You just repeat the clear line, calmly, like a broken record with excellent posture.

Try this:

Next time you feel that automatic "sure, no worries" rising to your lips, pause for three seconds. Ask yourself, "Do I actually want to agree to this as it is" If not, use one of the translation phrases from earlier and see what happens.

[2.9] THE POINT OF ALL THIS

This chapter isn't about turning you into a corporate politician who weighs every word like it's a press conference.

It's about:

- giving you language that matches reality
- shrinking the gap between your inner scream and your outer voice
- helping you say what matters without torching your career

This is basically translating your brain into workplace-safe English. Not fake, not fluffy, not corporate-speak, just clear and strategic. You're not trying to "win" conversations, you're trying to stop bleeding energy in every interaction. The goal is to be understood, stay employed, and keep your dignity, preferably all at the same time.

You don't have to nail this overnight.

If all you do this week is:

- say "I don't have capacity for that right now" once
- ask "what's the priority" instead of silently panicking
- or swap one "sure, no worries" for something more honest
- you're already changing the pattern.

In the next chapter, we're going to zoom in on the places that create most of the inner screaming: **meetings, emails and all the tiny daily torture devices** that eat your time and attention.

Chapter 3
Meetings, Emails And Other Daily Torture Devices

[3.1] Why Your Brain Feels Fried Before Lunch

You can have days where you barely touch your actual work, yet you finish completely wrecked.

You look back and realize you spent the day:

- sitting in meetings that bred more meetings
- answering emails about things nobody really cares about
- replying to chat messages that begin with "quick one" and are never quick

No wonder your brain's yelling "I cannot live like this" while your mouth says, *"Yep, all good."*

Modern work has turned into a game of:

- constant interruptions

- fake urgency

- everyone wanting an instant reply

Your nervous system never gets a proper break. You're always half alert, waiting for the next calendar invite or ping.

The brutal part is you're not tired from doing one hard thing. You're tired from switching between twenty tiny things all day. Every time you get pulled out of focus, your brain has to reboot, remember what you were doing, and pretend it's fine. It's like someone keeps slapping your hand off the steering wheel while you're driving, then acting confused when you're stressed. That constant context switching is what turns a normal workday into mental mush.

That's why this chapter exists. Not to magically erase meetings and emails, but to give you ways to:

- survive them
- reduce the nonsense
- protect your energy so you have something left for the work that actually matters

[3.2] MEETINGS: THE PLACE WHERE TIME GOES TO DIE

Let's talk about the worst offenders first.

There are good meetings. They:

- have a clear purpose
- have the right people
- end with decisions or actions

Then there's everything else.

You know the type:

- no agenda, no point, no end
- twelve people, three talk, everyone else checks email
- a long recap of stuff that could've been sent as a paragraph

Your inner voice in these meetings:

- "Why am I here?"
- "This could have been an email."
- "If we all left right now, would anything bad actually happen?"

On the outside you sip coffee, nod occasionally and say things like *"good point"* while your soul slowly leaves your body. You might not be able to avoid every useless meeting, but you can:

- question whether you actually need to be there
- nudge them to be less awful
- stop volunteering as the official note-taker for the clown show

[3.3] DO I REALLY NEED TO BE IN THIS MEETING

You're allowed to ask this question. Most people never do. They just accept every invite like it's a legal summons.

Before you hit accept, ask yourself:

- Do I actually need to contribute something here?
- Is there a decision that affects my work?
- Could I get what I need from the notes afterward?

If the answer is "no" to all of that, you at least have grounds to challenge or renegotiate.

You don't have to send, "This is pointless, take me off this." Tempting, but risky.

Try something like:

"Hey [Name], I saw the invite for [Meeting]. I'm keen to stay aligned, but I'm not sure I need to be in the full session. Would it work if I read the notes and jump in if you need me for anything specific?"

or

"At the moment I've got [X project] that needs focus. Are there parts of this meeting where you definitely need my input, or could I skip this one and catch up via notes?"

You're not saying "your meeting is stupid." You're saying "I want to use time well." Reasonable people respect that. Chronic meeting addicts might twitch, but that's their problem.

[3.4] MAKING MEETINGS SUCK LESS WHEN YOU'RE STUCK IN THEM

Sometimes you don't have a choice. You're in. You're not getting out. Fine. You can still make it less of a complete waste.

Here are a few small moves that change the vibe:

Ask for a purpose.
If a meeting feels aimless, you can say:

"Just so we're clear, what do we need to decide or achieve by the end of this?"

It sounds helpful, but it's really you saying, "What are we doing here exactly."

Ask for an agenda next time.
At the end of a chaotic meeting:

"For next time, could we send a short agenda ahead of time? It'll help everyone come prepared so we can move faster."

You're not shaming anyone. You're just planting a better habit.

Call time on the rambling.
If someone's giving a TED Talk about nothing helpful:

"We're a bit tight on time, so can we park that for now and come back if we need to?" or *"That's good context. To keep things moving, what's the decision you're proposing?"*

You don't have to do this every time. But once in a while, stepping in saves everyone ten minutes of their life.

[3.5] "CAMERA ON" AND OTHER MODERN TORTURE TRICKS

Online meetings added a fresh layer of weird. You now get:

- "Can you turn your camera on for engagement"
- ten people staring at their own face while pretending to listen
- chat messages that say, "You're on mute" every five minutes

You're allowed to protect yourself here too.

If having your camera on all day drains you, you can say:

"I'll keep my camera off for this one, I'm juggling a couple of things in the background, but I'm here and listening."

or

"My connection's a bit patchy so I'll stay audio only to keep things stable."

It's not a crime to have one meeting where you don't have to perform "interested face" on HD video.

You're also allowed to say:

"I won't be able to multitask properly in this meeting, so I might turn off notifications for a bit. If you need me urgently, call."

Translation: "I'm not going to answer every ping while you talk at me."

[3.6] EMAIL: THE NEVER-ENDING SLOT MACHINE

Email looks innocent until it isn't.

You open your inbox, intending to respond to one thing, and you're suddenly forty minutes deep in:

- pointless "reply all" chains
- vague requests with no details
- people forwarding chaos to you with "thoughts" as the entire message

Your inner voice:

- "Use a subject line like an adult."
- "What am I even supposed to do with this?"
- "Stop cc'ing me on your nonsense."

If you don't set any boundaries, your inbox will eat your whole day.

A few simple rules help a lot:

- **Batch email.** Pick 2 or 3 windows in the day to handle email. The rest of the time, close it. Completely.
- **Stop replying instantly.** You're training people to expect that you're always on and available. Most things can wait an hour.
- **Use subject lines properly.** You can't fix everyone else but you can at least make yours clear:

    - "[ACTION NEEDED] Approve X by Friday"
    - "[INFO] Notes from today's meeting"

[3.7] WRITING EMAILS THAT DON'T MAKE EVERYTHING WORSE

You don't have to write like a robot or a lawyer.
You do want to be:

- clear
- direct
- hard to misunderstand

Here are some quick patterns that keep you sane.

When you need clarity:
"To make sure we're on the same page, are you asking for [X] and by [when]?"

When someone sends a vague request:
"Happy to help. What does a good outcome look like for you here, and what's the deadline?"

When someone dumps something big on you with no time:
"I've got [X] and [Y] on my list already for today. If this is a higher priority, I can start it now and move one of those. Which should shift?"

When you want decisions in writing:
"Just confirming from our chat: you've chosen [Option A] and we're aiming for [date]. I'll move ahead on that basis."

These emails do a few important things at once:
- put ownership back where it belongs
- document what was agreed
- give you proof later when someone's memory suddenly gets selective

[3.8] CHAT APPS: PRODUCTIVITY OR CHAOS, DEPENDING HOW YOU USE THEM

Slack, Teams, whatever your flavor is, can be helpful. It can also turn your day into a live-action whack-a-mole.

If you treat every ping like a fire alarm, you'll never focus on anything real.

Some survival rules:

- **Mute channels that aren't critical.** You don't need a dopamine hit every time someone posts a meme.
- **Turn off pop up notifications for at least some of the day.** Check chat between tasks, not in the middle of them.
- **Use status messages.**
    - "Deep focus, responses slower."
    - "In back-to-back meetings, email for urgent."

You're not slacking off. You're making your brain usable for more than three minutes at a time.

When people abuse chat to throw work at you, lean on the same phrases from earlier:

"I've got a full plate right now, so I can't take this on. I can give you ten minutes to talk through next steps if that helps."
or
"For something this detailed, can you pop it in an email with the deadline and I'll pick it up in my next focus block."

You're training people not to treat you like a vending machine they can kick for instant results.

[3.9] Fake Urgency and the "Everything's Critical" Lie

One reason you scream in your head at work is simple:

Everything's "urgent."

You get emails marked high priority about things that absolutely are not.

You get chat messages with "ASAP" for tasks that could easily wait until tomorrow.

When everything's urgent, nothing is. It's just stress theater.

You're allowed to push back on fake urgency:

"I can get this done by [realistic time]. If it's truly urgent for today, I'll need to move [X]. Should I do that?"

If they say "no, that's fine," congrats, it was never urgent.

If they say "yes, move X," now the trade off's visible and it's their decision, not you silently absorbing the impact.

You can also ask:

"What happens if this isn't finished today?"

If the honest answer is "nothing terrible," it's not urgent. It's just someone else's anxiety.

[3.10] MICRO HACKS THAT GIVE YOU SOME BRAIN BACK

You're not going to fix your entire company's meeting culture alone. You can still give yourself a little space in the mess.

A few micro hacks:

- **Calendar blocking**
  Put fake meetings in your own calendar called things like "Focus" or "Deep work." If someone tries to schedule over everything, you can say, "I've already got something locked in then, can we try [other time]."

- **No meetings in the first or last hour**
  If you can influence your schedule at all, protect the start or end of your day from calls. Use it to plan, wrap up or just catch your breath.

- **Email templates**
  Save a few high quality replies you use a lot. Copy, tweak, send. Saves brain cells.

- **One screen at a time**
  When you're in a meeting, close your inbox. When you're writing, close chat. Multitasking feels productive and quietly murders your focus.

None of this is glamorous. It just nudges your day away from permanent reaction mode.

[3.11] WHEN THE SYSTEM'S THE PROBLEM, NOT YOUR TIME MANAGEMENT

It's easy to come out of a day of back-to-back meetings and think, "I'm so bad at managing my time."

Be careful.

Sometimes your time management could definitely use a tune up. Often though, the problem is:

- a culture that books meetings first and asks questions later

- leaders who treat email like a to do list they can write on for everyone else

- tools designed to interrupt you, not help you focus

You can always tweak your habits. You can't single handedly fix a company that treats constant availability as a personality trait.

So, when your brain starts in with "I'm so unproductive," try adding a line:

"Given the number of meetings and interruptions I'm dealing with, it's impressive I got anything done at all."

That doesn't mean you shrug and accept everything. It means you stop calling yourself useless for not thriving in a ridiculous setup.

[3.12] A SMALL EXPERIMENT FOR THE NEXT WEEK

You don't need a full productivity system. Try this tiny experiment instead.

For one week:
1. **Pick two email windows a day**
   For example, 10am and 3pm. The rest of the time, keep your inbox closed.
2. **Decline or renegotiate one meeting**
   Just one. Use one of the scripts from this chapter. See what happens.
3. **Use one clear phrase when work lands on your lap**
   For example, "What's the priority here?" or "What should I move to make space for this?"

At the end of the week, ask yourself:

- Did anything explode?
- Did I lose my job?
- Did anyone actually care as much as I feared?

Chances are, the world kept turning. You might even feel slightly less cooked.

That's the point of this chapter. Not to make your workplace perfect, but to turn down the daily torture devices enough that you can do your actual job and still have a brain left for your real life.

In the next chapter, we're going to look at **coworkers**. The legends, the nightmares and the walking red flags who feature heavily in the things you scream in your head at work.

CHAPTER 4
COWORKERS: LEGENDS, NIGHTMARES AND WALKING RED FLAGS

You can have a boring job that feels fine if the people are good.

You can have an interesting job that feels like hell if the people are awful.

Most of what you scream in your head at work is not about software or spreadsheets.

It is about **other humans**.

Because humans come with moods, egos, insecurities, and little invisible power games that have nothing to do with the actual work. One person can turn a simple task into a three-week drama series just by being vague, defensive, territorial, or weirdly competitive about a spreadsheet. Suddenly you're not "doing your job," you're managing feelings, decoding subtext, and translating nonsense into something actionable.

And the kicker is, the office rewards the loudest behavior, not the most useful behavior. The calm, competent people quietly carry the place, while the chaos merchants get airtime, attention, and promotions for "leadership energy." So, if you feel exhausted and irritated, you're not broken. You're reacting normally to a workplace that expects you to do work and babysit grown adults at the same time.

So, let's meet the cast of characters making your workday ten times harder than it needs to be:

- The legend who quietly saves the day.

- The coworker who creates chaos then disappears.

- The one who lives to argue in every meeting.

- The one who treats you like their personal assistant.

Your contract might list tasks and responsibilities. What you're actually doing is trying to get things done inside a very weird social experiment.

This chapter is about handling that experiment without losing your sanity.

[4.2] THE LEGENDS: PROTECT THEM AT ALL COSTS

Let's start with the good ones.

You know the type:

- They answer questions without making you feel stupid.
- They share information instead of hoarding it for power.
- They give credit.
- They quietly steer things away from disaster when someone higher up gets a wild idea.

These people are the reason you have not walked out yet. They are often just as tired and fed up as you, but they still try to do the right thing.

Your inner voice around them:
"Thank god you exist."

If you have even one or two of these, treat them like the rare resource they are.

How to look after that relationship:

- Say thank you clearly, not just in your head.
- Share useful info back, do not only take.
- Defend them when someone tries to throw them under the bus.
- If you leave, help them if you can. They probably deserve better too.

You don't have to love your job. Having one decent coworker makes it survivable.

[4.3] THE ENERGY VAMPIRE

Then there is the other type. The one who appears at your desk or in your DMs and suddenly:

- you're listening to a 25-minute rant
- you've agreed to help with something you do not own
- your brain feels like it has been wrung out

They might not be a bad person. They are just an **energy vampire**. They feed on your attention, your time and your emotional labor.

Signs you're dealing with one:

- You feel drained after talking to them.
- Every conversation is about their problems.
- They never actually act on advice; they just want to vent again tomorrow.
- They appear whenever you're obviously busy.

You're allowed to protect yourself, even if they mean well.

Simple boundaries:

"I've only got five minutes, then I need to get back to this."
or
"I get that it's frustrating. I've got to finish this now. Maybe talk to [manager/HR/friend] about it properly."

You're not their therapist. You're not the complaint department. You're another tired employee trying not to fall apart.

[4.4] THE SLACKER WHO SOMEHOW GETS AWAY WITH EVERYTHING

You know this one too.

They float around, doing the bare minimum while:
- missing deadlines
- showing up unprepared
- dropping tasks on others at the last minute

Then when things go well, they are right there to smile and say *"we did it."*

Your inner voice:
"We? What do you mean we."

You cannot single handedly fix someone's work ethic, but you can stop quietly carrying their load.

The reason they "somehow get away with it" is usually boring, not magical. They've mastered the art of looking busy, saying the right vague things, and being just pleasant enough that nobody wants the awkward conversation. Meanwhile, you and the other competent people step in to keep the wheels on, because you care, you hate mess, and you don't want to be the reason something fails. Congrats. That's exactly how slackers survive.

They also thrive in workplaces where ownership is fuzzy. If tasks live in someone's head, or in a meeting that was never written down, the slacker can always claim confusion. "Oh, I thought you had that." "I didn't see that message." "I was waiting on feedback." Suddenly the delay becomes a group problem instead of their problem. The slacker's favorite habitat is a workplace with no receipts.

So, the move is not to shame them or try to motivate them. The move is to make the work visible. Make responsibility visible. Make timelines visible. If it's clear who owns what and when, they can still slack, but they can't do it in the dark. You're not escalating. You're turning the lights on.

And yes, the first time you stop catching their dropped balls, it might feel like you're being "petty." You're not. You're being accurate. If the team has been propping them up for months, your boundary will feel like a disruption. Let it. The short-term discomfort is better than a long-term career as the unofficial backup employee for someone who can't be bothered.

Practical moves:

- Stop agreeing to "just help out" every time.
- Document who owns what in shared tasks.
- Use written follow ups that clearly show responsibility.

Example email:

"Great, so you'll handle the first draft of the report by Thursday and I'll do the data check on Friday. If anything changes on your side, let me know so I can move my timing."

Later, if anyone asks why something is late, you can calmly say:
"I was scheduled to do the data check once the draft came through. I did not receive that until [date], so I started then."

You're not throwing them under the bus. You're refusing to lie down in front of it.

[4.5] THE GOSSIP MACHINE

A little gossip is normal. You're not a robot, and sometimes people need to vent.

The problem is the person who:
- knows everyone's business
- lives for drama
- always has "inside info"
- mysteriously causes tension wherever they go

You might think staying close to them keeps you safe. It does the opposite. You're one minor conflict away from being their next story.

Warning signs:
- They share things other people told them in confidence.
- They talk trash about people they claim to like.
- They bring you "updates" that make you dislike someone you've never personally had trouble with.

You don't have to announce, *"I'm not going to gossip with you anymore."* You can just stop feeding the fire.

Things you can say:

"I'm trying to stay out of that stuff to be honest." or *"I have not had that experience with them, so I can't really say."*

Then change the subject to work. Boring? Yes. Safer? Also, yes.

If someone gossips to you constantly, remember: If they do it with you, they do it about you.

[4.6] THE MICROMANAGER IN COWORKER CLOTHING

Sometimes the issue is not your boss. It's the coworker who acts like they are your boss.

They:
- check up on you constantly
- tell you how to do tasks you know perfectly well
- insert themselves into things you did not ask them to manage

Your inner voice:
- "I didn't ask for a second manager."
- What you need here is a calm, firm reset.

You can try:
"I've got this one covered. If I need a second pair of eyes, I'll let you know."
or
"Appreciate the input. I'll take it from here and flag anything I need help on."

If they keep hovering:
"I work best when I can run with my part. If there's feedback, can we do it once at the end instead of step by step? It'll be more efficient."

You're not picking a fight. You're telling them how to work with you like an adult.

[4.7] THE PASSIVE AGGRESSIVE "NICE" COWORKER

Some coworkers never say anything directly. They operate in hints and tones:

- "Wow, must be nice leaving on time."
- "I guess some of us are just busier than others."
- "I would have done it differently, but if you're happy with it…"

Your brain:

"Say what you actually mean or shut up."

You don't have to swallow every little dig. You also don't have to match their passive aggression.

You can try bringing it into the open:

"It sounds like you've got some concerns. Do you want to say them directly so we can sort it out?"

or, if they make a "joke" at your expense:

"If there's something you're unhappy with, tell me straight. I'd rather that than side comments."

A lot of passive aggressive people back off when they realize, you're not an easy target. They want low effort shots, not actual conversations.

[4.8] THE WALKING RED FLAG

Some coworkers are not just annoying. They are dangerous to your peace, your reputation or sometimes your safety.

Red flags include:

- They love stirring conflict, then stepping back to watch.
- They take credit for your work.
- They blame you for their mistakes.
- They lie or twist events to make themselves look better.
- They push boundaries, comments, or "jokes" that feel gross or targeted.

Your job isn't to diagnose them, it's to **limit their access to your life**.

Practical steps:

- Keep important interactions in writing. Follow up verbal agreements with short recap emails.
- Avoid sharing personal information they can weaponize.
- Don't vent to them about other coworkers. They will use it if it benefits them.

If they cross a serious line, document it. Write down dates, times, what was said, who was there. If you need HR later, you will be grateful you did.

You're not being paranoid. You're looking after yourself in a place where not everyone is on your team.

[4.9] BEING A DECENT COWORKER YOURSELF

Here's the bit nobody likes hearing: some of the behavior you hate in others, you might be doing too when you're tired, stressed, or on autopilot.

You don't have to be perfect. It does help to not be part of the problem.

Quick self-check:
- Do you regularly dump last minute tasks on others because you left things late?
- Do you say "yes" and then secretly resent people instead of being honest about your limits?
- Do you vent about coworkers more than you talk to them directly?
- Do you take over tasks because you think you'll do them better, then get bitter that no one helps you?

If you see yourself in some of that, welcome to being human. Just do a bit better where you can.

Simple ways to be less of an idiot at work:

- Give people context, not just requests.
- Say thank you. Out loud. Often.
- Don't cc someone's boss to "make a point" unless it's serious.
- If you're frustrated, sleep on the email. Read it again tomorrow.

You can be honest, pissed off, and funny without making life harder for people who don't deserve it.

[4.10] PICKING YOUR BATTLES

You will never fix every annoying coworker. If that's your goal, you'll burn out trying.

Instead, aim for this:

- Decide who's worth your time.
- Decide what's worth your energy.
- Let some stuff go on purpose.

Ask yourself:

- Is this a one off or a pattern?
- Does this actually affect my work, or is it just irritating?
- Will I care about this a week from now?

If it's a pattern and it affects your work, it may be worth a direct conversation or a boundary.

If it's someone chewing loudly in a meeting, maybe you take a deep breath and save your energy for something that matters.

Your inner voice will still scream. It's allowed to. You don't need to act on every internal scream like it's a mission from the universe.

[4.11] BUILDING TINY ALLIANCES

You don't need a whole army. You just need a few people who:

- tell you the truth
- share information
- are not secretly trying to screw you over

You don't have to become best friends. You just build small, solid alliances.

How:

- Share something useful with no strings attached.
- Back them up in meetings when they make a good point.
- Give them credit openly when they help you.

Example:

"That idea came from [Name] originally, I just built on it."

or

"[Name] flagged this risk last week, which really helped us avoid a mess."

Decent people remember who had their back. Over time, you end up with a quiet network of coworkers who are more likely to support you when you need it.

[4.12] WHEN YOU ACTUALLY NEED TO ESCALATE

Sometimes, after you've tried all the normal adult things:

- setting boundaries
- being clear
- staying calm

the coworker still keeps crossing lines.

That's when you start thinking about escalation. Not because you love drama, but because you've run out of lower-level options.

Before you go to a manager or HR:

- Write down specific incidents. Dates, times, what was said or done.
- Focus on impact on the work and the team, not just "I hate this person."
- Decide what you want to ask for; A mediated conversation, A change in how work is assigned; A seat change

When you do raise it, keep it simple:

"I want to flag a pattern that's affecting my ability to do my job. Here are three examples. I've tried [X and Y] already. I'm asking for [Z]."

If your manager shrugs and says "that's just how they are," that tells you something important about the culture you're in. Make a note of it for your future exit plan.

[4.13] A SMALL EXERCISE: MAPPING YOUR PEOPLE

Grab a scrap of paper or open a blank note and write down three columns:

- "Keeps me sane"
- "Neutral but fine"
- "Drains me"

Put initials, not full names. You're not getting this tattooed.

- *Under* "Keeps me sane," list the legends who make work less awful.
- *Under* "Neutral but fine," put the people who are just doing their thing.
- *Under* "Drains me," list the ones who suck your energy or cause most of your inner screaming.

Now ask:

- Can I spend slightly more time and attention on the first group?
- Can I keep the middle group steady?
- Can I reduce unprotected exposure to the last group, even by 10 percent?

That might look like:

- eating lunch with the sane ones more often
- putting headphones on near the energy vampire
- moving more conversations with a red flag coworker into written channels

One more thing: pay attention to **how** the draining people drain you. Are they draining because they interrupt, because they dump work, because they gossip, because they nitpick, or because they make everything emotionally weird? Write one word next to each initial, like "interrupts," "drama," "dumps," "micromanages," or "guilt." That tiny label helps you choose the right defense instead of just absorbing the vibe and feeling miserable.

Then pick one "drains me" person and run a simple test for a week: **move them one step further away from your time and attention.** Not a dramatic confrontation. Just fewer calls, more written updates, fewer instant replies, shorter conversations, and more "I've got to jump" exits. You're not punishing them. You're reducing dosage. Think of it like limiting junk food. You can still have it. You just don't want it as your main diet.

Finally, protect the "keeps me sane" list like its oxygen. A five-minute chat with the right person can undo an hour of workplace nonsense. If you have even one legend, keep that connection alive. When the day is stupid, those small sane moments are how you remember you're not the crazy one.

You're not going to redesign your entire org chart. You're just shifting the balance so your day contains more humans who keep you human, and fewer who make you want to scream into a pillow.

In the next chapter, we're going to talk about the people who technically run the show: **managers, HR and the beautiful lie that "we're a family."**

Chapter 5
Managers, HR And The "We're A Family" Lie

Coworkers annoy you. Managers and HR change your life.

A good manager can:
- shield you from nonsense
- fight for fair workload
- give you credit and cover your back

A bad one can:
- throw you under the nearest bus
- pretend your burnout is a "mindset issue"
- use HR like a threat, not a support

Your inner voice around this stuff is usually loud:

- "You have no idea what you're doing."
- "Stop telling me it's fine, it's not fine."
- "We are not a family. I'm here because you pay me."

Managers and HR don't just affect your workload. They control the invisible stuff that decides whether work feels safe or stressful: clarity, expectations, boundaries, and consequences. When that leadership layer is decent, you can handle a lot. When it's chaotic, passive aggressive, or ego-driven, even small tasks feel like walking through a minefield with a smile.

Also, most workplace misery isn't caused by one dramatic blow-up. It's death by a thousand tiny power moves. Vague feedback. Shifting goalposts. Praise in private, blame in public. "Let's circle back" as a delay tactic. "Just checking in" as a threat in a cardigan. It's not always loud. Sometimes it's quietly toxic, which is almost worse because you start questioning your own reality.

So, the goal here is not "become best friends with leadership" or "win the office." It's to understand the patterns, protect yourself, and respond in ways that don't accidentally make you the easiest target. You're not trying to out-politic the politicians. You're trying to survive their nonsense without handing them extra ammunition.

This chapter is here to help you deal with the people who sign off performance reviews, sit in leadership meetings and post inspirational quotes on LinkedIn while you quietly lose your mind.

[5.2] "WE'RE A FAMILY" IS A RED FLAG IN A BLAZER

If you've ever heard someone at work say, "We're not just a company, we're a family," your inner voice probably screamed.

At home, "family" means unconditional love, loyalty and helping each other even when it's inconvenient.

At work, "family" often means:

- work ridiculous hours because "we're all in this together"

- ignore bad behavior because "that's just how they are"

- feel guilty for wanting better pay, boundaries or to leave

You're not your manager's child. They're not your parent. You're in a **transaction**. You give labor. They give money. Everything else is decoration.

You can care about your colleagues deeply. You can enjoy your work. You can still say, very clearly in your head:

"This is not my family. This is my job."

When you remember that, it's easier to make decisions that protect you, not just the company's feelings.

Not every manager is evil. A lot are simply out of their depth, untrained, or too scared to push back at the people above them.

Some common species:

The Ghost

They're never available. They dodge questions. They say "good work team" and vanish.

Result: you drift with no guidance, then get surprised feedback at review time.

The Buddy

They want to be everyone's friend. They avoid conflict. They never give hard feedback.

Result: issues rot under the surface until something explodes.

The Control Freak

They want updates on everything. They rewrite your work "to be safe." They don't trust anyone.

Result: you feel watched, small and stuck at apprentice level forever.

The Hero

They take on everything. They swoop in to "rescue" projects. They brag about working insane hours.

Result: they teach the team that burning out is noble and boundaries are for the weak.

The Politician

They manage upwards beautifully, say all the right things to leadership, and quietly throw you under the bus when targets are missed.

Result: you become the shield for their reputation.

You might recognize flavors of a few in your own manager. None of them mean you're powerless. They just mean you need different tactics.

The tricky part is most of these managers don't *look* toxic at first. They look busy, friendly, "high standards," or "super committed." The damage shows up later, in your stress levels and your workload, not in one dramatic moment. They create confusion, churn, and pressure, then act shocked when you're fried. It's like being slowly boiled while someone says, *"You doing okay in there?"*

Also, notice how almost every type has the same hidden effect: **you do more emotional labor.** You chase clarity from the Ghost. You manage conflict for the Buddy. You babysit the Control Freak's anxiety. You clean up after the Hero's chaos. You become the Politician's human shield. You're not just doing your job. You're compensating for theirs.

So, your goal isn't to diagnose them like a workplace therapist. Your goal is to protect your time, get expectations in writing, and stop being the default solution to their weaknesses. In the next sections, we'll turn these "species" into practical tactics you can actually use, without starting a war you don't have time for.

[5.4] HOW TO MAKE A USELESS ONE SLIGHTLY MORE USEFUL

You probably can't transform your manager into your dream leader. You can often nudge them into being less useless.

Start by getting clear on what you actually need:
- clear priorities
- realistic timelines
- feedback that's specific, not vague vibes
- support when there's conflict or overload

Then make those needs ridiculously explicit.

You can say:
"To make sure I'm focusing on the right things, can we agree my top three priorities for this week?"
or
"Feedback really helps me. Can you give me one thing that's going well and one thing I can improve on in this project?"
or
"I'm at capacity right now. I need your help deciding what moves if we add this new piece of work."

You're teaching them how to manage you. You're not waiting for them to magically guess what you need.

If they give vague feedback like *"you just need to be more proactive,"* you can push back gently:

"I want to improve. Can you give me a concrete example of what 'more proactive' would look like in my role?"

If they can't answer, that's their lack of clarity, not your failure.

[5.5] PERFORMANCE REVIEWS AND OTHER ANXIETY FESTIVALS

Performance reviews are where a lot of people's inner screaming hits maximum volume.

You sit there thinking:

- "Please don't blindside me."
- "Please don't say something vague and unhelpful."
- "Please just acknowledge all the work I did while everything was on fire."

You can't control the review, but you can:

- go in prepared
- have your own receipts
- steer the conversation a bit

Before review time, make yourself a simple brag sheet:

- projects you completed
- fires you put out
- positive feedback you got from others (emails, messages, comments)
- ways you went beyond your basic job description

Also, don't wait until review time to find out what the story is. A few weeks before reviews, book a quick check-in and ask one simple question: *"What would make you say this was a strong period for me?"*. That forces them to name expectations while there's still time to meet them. It also reduces the chance you walk into the review and discover your manager has been quietly building a little fantasy narrative in their head.

And if you can, collect one or two outside voices. Send a short message to someone you worked with: "Hey, quick one, I'm putting together my review notes. Is there anything you think I did well on this project?". You're not fishing for compliments. You're gathering proof. In a messy workplace, whoever has the clearest receipts usually wins the "how did this period go?" conversation.

Then, in the meeting, you can say:

"Here are some highlights I'm proud of this period."

You're not being arrogant. You're reminding them of things they've probably forgotten. Managers see a lot. You need to make your impact easy to remember.

If you get feedback that feels unfair or inaccurate, breathe. Try:

"I wasn't aware that was a concern, so I'd like to understand it better. Can you share a specific example so I know what to work on?"

If they can't, you've quietly flagged that their criticism is fuzzy.

You don't have to agree with everything, but arguing every point rarely ends well. Take what's useful, note what's nonsense, and remember that one person's opinion is not the full truth about you.

[5.6] HR: HELP, HARM, OR CORPORATE PR

Here's the thing nobody in HR is allowed to put on their posters. HR's primary client is the company, not you.

Good HR people genuinely care about employees. They want things to be fair, safe and not completely chaotic. But at the end of the day, they're paid to:

- protect the organization
- reduce legal risk
- uphold policy

That doesn't mean you should never go to HR. It means you should be strategic about **when** and **how** you do it.

Also, don't expect HR to behave like a personal therapist or a justice system. Their usual playbook is: listen, document, check policy, and aim for the lowest-drama solution that stops the problem from becoming a bigger problem. Sometimes that means real action. Sometimes it means "coaching." Sometimes it means quietly protecting the person who brings in money or has power. It's not always fair, but it is predictable once you understand what game they're playing.

Your best weapon with HR is not emotion, it's clarity and a paper trail. If you have a conversation in person, follow up with an email that politely summarizes what was discussed and what the next steps are. Not in a dramatic way. Just: "Thanks for speaking with me today. To confirm, we discussed [X], and the next step is [Y]." If things later get twisted, minimized, or "forgotten," that written summary becomes your anchor.

Good times to involve HR:

- serious harassment or discrimination
- bullying that hasn't changed after you raised it
- pay issues that aren't getting resolved
- clear policy violations

Bad times:

- you're annoyed with your coworker
- your manager hurt your feelings once
- you want someone to be "told off" for being annoying

Before you go to HR, get your story clear:

- what happened
- when it happened
- who was there
- what you've already tried to fix it

You're not going in to "vent." You're going in to report something specific.

You can say:

"I'm raising this because it's affecting my ability to do my job and I don't feel safe or comfortable handling it alone."

If HR's useful, great. If they're clearly just protecting the company and sweeping things under the rug, that's an important data point for your exit plan.

[5.7] WHEN YOUR MANAGER IS PART OF THE PROBLEM

Sometimes the main source of inner screaming is not "work" in general. It's one person with power over your day.

Maybe they:

- take credit for your work
- call you at all hours
- belittle you in front of others
- ignore your concerns completely

You're not obliged to accept that as normal.

Start small:

- Move important conversations into writing.
- Summarize verbal agreements in follow up emails:

"Just to confirm what we agreed in today's check in, I'll do [X] by [date] and you'll handle [Y]."

Keep a private record of concerning behavior with dates, times, and quotes while it's fresh.

One important note: with a decent manager, a direct conversation can fix things quickly. With a toxic one, it can turn into a weird little court case where they argue your feelings, question your intent, or punish you later in subtle ways. So don't go in hoping for an apology and a character arc. Go in aiming for one thing only: a clear request, a clear boundary, and a clear record of what happened next.

Also, don't have that conversation in the most vulnerable way possible. Pick a calm time, keep it short, and keep it specific. If you can, follow up afterward with a neutral email summary: "Thanks for chatting today. To confirm, we agreed [X] going forward." That way you're not relying on their memory, their mood, or their ability to rewrite history when it suits them.

Then, if you feel safe enough, try a direct conversation:

"I want to talk about something that's been bothering me. When [specific behavior] happens, I feel [effect]. I'd like us to [specific change]."

Example:

"When I get messages late at night about non urgent things, I feel like I'm expected to be available 24/7. I'd like us to keep non urgent requests to work hours where possible."

You're not saying "you're a monster." You're naming behavior and asking for a change.

If that goes nowhere, or makes things worse, that's when you start considering:

- escalation to their manager or HR
- moving internally
- speeding up your external job search

Your mental and physical health are worth more than keeping one bad manager happy.

[5.8] THE MYTH OF LOYALTY

You've probably been fed some version of:

- "We value loyalty here."
- "We look after people who stick it out."
- "You've been here so long, you're part of the furniture."

Loyalty in practice often means:

- you do more work than you're paid for
- you stay years past the use by date
- you feel guilty for even looking at other jobs

Here's the uncomfortable truth:

If it suits the business, they'll restructure, downsize or "move in a different direction" and your loyalty won't save you.

That doesn't mean you should be a selfish gremlin. It means:

- *be loyal* to your values
- *be loyal* to your health
- *be loyal* to your own future

Loyalty is fine when it goes both ways. When it doesn't, you're allowed to stop treating your job like a marriage and start treating it like what it is: an arrangement that works until it doesn't.

[5.9] WHEN YOU'RE THE ONE IN CHARGE

You might be reading this as someone who manages others and thinking, "God, I hope this isn't how my team feels about me."

Good. That means you care. Quick gut check:
- *Do you* protect your team from random drive by requests, or just pass them down?
- *Do you* give clear priorities, or dump everything and say "figure it out"?
- *Do you* listen when they say something isn't sustainable, or tell them to "push through"?
- *Do you* take blame when things go wrong, or instantly look for someone to blame?

You're going to screw up sometimes. Own it. People will forgive almost anything if they feel you're honest and on their side.

Simple things that make you less of a nightmare boss:

- Say "thank you" specifically.
- Ask "what do you need from me to make this doable" instead of "can you just get it done"
- Don't discuss one team member's performance with another. They will assume you do the same to them.
- When you say "log off and rest," mean it. Don't then reward the people who ignore you and keep working.

If you care about not being the villain in someone else's workplace trauma story, you're already ahead of half the managers out there.

[5.10] ACCEPTING WHAT YOU CAN'T FIX FROM THE MIDDLE

You're not the CEO. You're not magically rewiring the entire company culture from your desk.

You can:

- set boundaries
- speak up when it matters
- document and protect yourself
- treat people decently on your level

You probably can't:

- make your manager emotionally intelligent
- turn HR into a therapy service
- convince leadership to suddenly value people over profits

That gap between what you want to change and what you actually can change is where a lot of the screaming in your head comes from.

It helps to separate:

- "This sucks and I can do something about it."
- "This sucks and I can't fix it from here."

For the first group, use the scripts, boundaries and tiny rebellions from this book.

Here's the mindset shift that stops you spiraling: you're not failing because you can't fix the whole system. You're just a person inside a system. A weird, messy system that often rewards nonsense. Your job is not to save it. Your job is to survive it with your sanity intact and your self-respect still in one piece.

Also, "accepting" isn't the same as tolerating. Accepting means you stop negotiating with reality. You stop thinking, "If I just explain it one more time, they'll finally get it." Some workplaces don't ever "get it". Some leaders don't learn. When you accept that, you stop wasting emotional energy on imaginary outcomes and start making practical moves.

And if this part stings, good. That sting is information. It's your brain telling you, "This place is not built for the kind of work life I want." You can still do your job professionally while you quietly reposition yourself for better. That's not drama. That's strategy.

For the second, start quietly moving your energy into:

- things that matter outside work
- skills that make you more employable
- building your network so you have options

It's not giving up. It's choosing where to spend your limited energy instead of smashing yourself against a wall.

[5.11] A SMALL REALITY CHECK BEFORE WE MOVE ON

If you've ever walked out of a one-on-one with your manager or a chat with HR and thought:

- "Am I crazy?"
- "Did that actually just happen?"
- "Why do I feel worse than before I asked for help?"

you're not alone.

You're working inside systems that were not built for your wellbeing. You're dealing with people who have their own insecurities, blind spots and incentives.

That "feeling worse" part is a big clue. When you raise something reasonable and walk away doubting your own reality, it usually means the conversation was designed to manage you, not help you. Vague answers, polite deflection, "we'll look into it," and subtle blame-shifting can mess with your head because it sounds supportive while changing nothing. So, if you leave confused, drained, or quietly furious, trust that reaction. It's your internal warning system doing its job.

Your job is not to fix all of that. Your job is to:

- stay awake to what's really going on
- stop taking all the blame for broken systems
- look after yourself and the people who deserve it

In the next chapter, we'll get into the part most toxic workplaces hate the idea of: **boundaries, micro rebellions and staying human** in a place that treats you like a resource.

88

CHAPTER 6
BOUNDARIES, MICRO REBELLIONS AND STAYING HUMAN

[6.1] BOUNDARIES ARE NOT RUDE, THEY'RE SURVIVAL

Workplaces love people with "no boundaries." They call them:

- dedicated
- loyal
- team players

What they really mean is:

- available at all hours
- says yes to everything
- burns out quietly without making a fuss

If you're reading this, there's a good chance you've been that person. You stay late. You pick up the slack. You answer messages you shouldn't. You tell yourself, "It's just for now," while "now" stretches into years.

The reason boundaries feel hard isn't because you're weak. It's because you've probably been trained to think that being liked equals being safe. So, you over-deliver, over-explain, and over-compensate, just in case someone decides you're "not committed enough." In a toxic workplace, that fear gets weaponized. The moment you hesitate; someone acts like you've personally cancelled Christmas.

Here's the truth: boundaries don't make you a problem. They make you predictable. They stop your work from being shaped by whoever shouts the loudest or panics the most. When you protect your time, you actually do better work, because you're not constantly drowning. So, the goal is not to become cold or uncaring. The goal is to stop donating your life to people who wouldn't even notice if you disappeared for a week.

Your brain screams:
"I can't keep doing this."

Your mouth says:
"Yeah, I can take that on."

Boundaries are the bridge between those two. They're not about being difficult. They're about staying human in a place that's very happy to treat you like a rechargeable battery.

[6.2] WHAT A BOUNDARY ACTUALLY IS (AND ISN'T)

A boundary is:

- where your responsibility ends and someone else's begins
- what you will and won't do
- what you will and won't tolerate

A boundary is **not**:

- a threat
- a tantrum
- a one-time dramatic announcement

It's a repeated behavior that says, "This is my line."

For example:

- "I don't answer non urgent work messages after 6pm"
- "I won't take on new projects without a clear deadline and priority."
- "I won't accept being spoken to with sarcasm or disrespect in front of others."

You don't have to give a TED Talk about your boundaries. You just have to behave like they're real.

[6.3] WHY YOU FEEL GUILTY SETTING THEM

If you've spent years being "the reliable one," setting boundaries will feel wrong at first.

You'll think:

- "They'll be disappointed."

- "They'll think I'm lazy now."

- "What if they get mad and fire me?"

Reality check:

- People will absolutely be disappointed if they benefited from you having no boundaries.

- They might think you're "less easy" now. That's fine. You're not a vending machine.

- If a company fires you for having basic human limits, it was never safe to begin with.

The guilt is normal. It doesn't mean the boundary's wrong. It means you're unlearning a role that never should've been yours in the first place.

[6.4] TIME BOUNDARIES: WHEN THE DAY ACTUALLY ENDS

Let's start with the obvious one: time.

Signs your time boundaries are wrecked:

- You regularly work past your finish time "just to catch up."
- You check email or chat one last time before bed. And then again.
- You feel an urge to reply instantly, even to things that can clearly wait.

You can't always control the hours you're rostered, but you can control how much unpaid overtime you hand over like free candy.

Simple time boundaries:

- **Pick a cut off**
  "I stop looking at work stuff after 6pm"

- **Delay sends**
  Write replies if you must, schedule them for the morning. People learn you're not instantly available.

- **Use out of office or status**
  "Offline for the evening, I'll reply tomorrow."

If you're in a culture where everyone brags about being online all night, this will feel rebellious. Good. That's the point.

[6.5] WORKLOAD BOUNDARIES: WHEN YOUR PLATE IS FULL

You don't have an infinite plate. You have a normal sized human plate and twelve people trying to stack projects on it.

Every time you say *"sure, I'll make it work"* when you're already at capacity, you're telling the system, "This is fine."

Start using phrases like:

"I'm at full capacity with [X, Y, and Z]. If this is higher priority, I can take it on and move one of those. Which should shift?"

or

"I can do this by [realistic date]. If it needs to be sooner, who can we bring in to help?"

You're not refusing. You're refusing to pretend you can do two jobs for the price of one.

Will some managers still try to load you up anyway, probably. That's why you document it. Then when someone asks why something slipped, you can calmly say:

"At the time, we agreed [new urgent thing] was the priority, so [other thing] moved."

You're not throwing a tantrum. You're refusing to be the silent sponge for everyone else's lack of or bad planning.

[6.6] EMOTIONAL BOUNDARIES: YOU'RE NOT A SPONGE

If you're halfway decent, people will naturally come to you to vent. That's fine, up to a point.

But if:

- you're carrying your own stress
- plus your coworker's problems
- plus your manager's anxiety
- plus the whole team's mood

you're going to feel like a walking stress bin.

You're allowed to say:

"I get that this is a lot. I've got a full brain myself at the moment, so I don't have much capacity to unpack it properly with you."

or

"I'm on your side, but I'm not the right person to fix this. Have you spoken to [manager/HR/professional]"

You're not heartless. You're just refusing to be the unpaid therapist for an organization that probably has an Employee Assistance Program somewhere collecting dust.

[6.7] Micro Rebellions: Tiny Ways to Stop Feeling Like a Robot

You can't always launch a massive protest. You can build in **micro rebellions** that remind you you're still a person with a spine.

These aren't about getting fired. They're about getting a tiny bit of yourself back.

Examples:

- Taking your full lunch break away from your desk without apologizing.

- Saying *"I can't do that today"* instead of *"I'll try."*

- Closing your laptop at finish time even when others stay logged in.

- Using your annual leave instead of saving it "for the right time" that never comes.

- Pushing your chair back in a pointless meeting and turning your camera off for five minutes to breathe.

Tiny, yes. But each one is a small "no" to the idea that your only purpose is to grind until you drop.

[6.8] RITUALS THAT KEEP YOU HUMAN

Toxic workplaces blur the lines between "you at work" and "you as an actual human being."

You start:

- dreaming about work
- checking email in the bathroom
- talking to friends and family mostly about your job

You need little rituals that remind your brain, "This is my life. Work's just one part."

Some ideas:

Transition ritual after work
Put your phone on a shelf, change clothes, go for a ten-minute walk, anything that signals, "Work mode off."

A no work talk rule for part of the evening
For one hour, you're not allowed to talk about your job. If you live alone, this still counts. Talk to yourself about anything else.

A small thing that's just for you
Reading, gaming, gardening, trash TV, walking the dog. Something that doesn't make money and doesn't go on a performance review.

These things look silly when you're exhausted. They're not. They're how you remember you exist outside the role.

[6.9] SAYING "NO" WITHOUT WRITING AN ESSAY

If you're used to overexplaining, you'll feel like you need a three-paragraph justification every time you say no.

You don't.

Short "no" templates:

- "I can't take that on right now with my current workload."
- "I'm not able to stay late this evening."
- "That's outside my role, so I'll have to say no to owning it."
- "I don't have capacity for that, but I can suggest [alternative]."

Notice what's missing:

- huge explanations
- personal apologies
- promises to "make it up"

Also, expect the follow-up guilt trip. "Just this once?" "It'll only take five minutes." "But you're the best person for it." That's where most people cave, not because they changed their mind, but because they got uncomfortable. Your move is to repeat the same sentence with slightly different packaging. No new reasons. No fresh excuses. Just calm repetition. If you keep feeding them explanations, they'll keep trying to debate them.

You're allowed to have a limit without writing an essay about why it exists.

[6.10] WHEN YOUR BOUNDARY GETS TESTED (AND IT WILL)

People don't believe a boundary is real the first time you say it. They believe it when they see what happens after they push it.

Example:

You say:
"I don't answer non urgent messages after 6pm"

Then someone messages you at 7pm and you respond straight away anyway.

Your boundary just evaporated in front of them. They learned, "Oh, that was just words."

And yes, it can feel risky at first. Your brain starts running disaster movies like: "What if they get mad?" "What if I'm labeled difficult?" Here's the reality: most people aren't shocked that you have a boundary. They're shocked you're enforcing it. If you're nervous, start with a soft version: don't reply instantly. Wait. Reply the next morning. Train the expectation slowly. Boundaries don't have to arrive with fireworks. They just have to show up consistently.

If you want it to stick:
- Don't reply. Answer in work hours.
- If they mention it later, you can say:

"Yeah, I was offline then. If it's urgent in future, call. Otherwise, I'll see it the next day."

You don't have to be aggressive. You just have to be consistent.

[6.11] WHEN YOU'RE SCARED TO SET BOUNDARIES BECAUSE YOU NEED THE JOB

This is real. You're not imagining it. Some workplaces punish anyone who doesn't act like a martyr.

You might be thinking:

- "Easy for you to say, I can't afford to make waves."
- "I'm on a visa/probation/short contract, and I can't risk it."
- "I've seen what happens to people who push back."

In those situations, your boundaries might need to be smaller and quieter, but they still matter.

You might not be able to refuse a task outright, but you can:

- protect your evenings two nights a week instead of none
- push for realistic deadlines on smaller tasks
- say "I'll start this tomorrow morning" instead of dropping everything instantly

You might not announce your boundaries formally, you can:

- keep records of overload
- quietly look for other roles
- treat this job as a stepping stone, not your permanent home

You're not weak for staying. You're not wrong for needing the paycheck. Just don't let "I need this job" turn into "I'll accept anything."

[6.12] BEING KIND TO YOURSELF WHEN YOU SLIP

You're going to mess this up. You'll say yes when you meant no. You'll answer messages at 11pm. You'll stay late again and hate yourself on the drive home.

Beating yourself up doesn't help. That just adds more noise in your head.

Also, slipping doesn't mean your boundary was fake. It means you're unlearning a habit you've practiced for years: people pleasing, panic responding, and trying to prove you're "easy to work with." Toxic workplaces train you to treat every request like a fire alarm. So, when you catch yourself doing the old thing, don't turn it into a personality defect. Just treat it like data. "Okay, that's my default setting. Let's update it."

Instead, try:
"Okay, I slipped that time. Next time I'll try [different response]."

Think of boundaries like a muscle. You're not weak because you can't lift the heaviest weight on day one. You build up gradually.

Celebrate tiny wins:
- the time you declined a meeting
- the email where you asked for a realistic deadline
- the moment you closed your laptop at finish time and actually walked away

Those are small, but they're how you claw your life back one inch at a time.

[6.13] A TINY REBELLION CHALLENGE

Pick **one** micro rebellion from this list for the next week:

- Take your full lunch break away from your screen at least three days.
- Turn off push notifications for email or chat outside work hours.
- Say "I don't have capacity for that right now" once.
- Put one thing back on someone else's list instead of silently absorbing it.

Treat it like a low stakes science experiment, not a personality makeover. You're not trying to become a new person by Monday. You're just testing what happens when you stop auto yes-ing. Pay attention to the reaction you get too. If someone gets weirdly upset about a basic boundary, that tells you a lot about how much they were benefiting from you having none.

At the end of the week, ask yourself:

- Did the world end?
- Did anyone truly lose their mind?
- Did I feel even slightly more like a human and less like a machine?

If the answer to that last one is yes, that's what a boundary does. It gives you back a piece of yourself.

In the next chapter, we'll turn from survival mode to improvement mode and look at **how to make work slightly less awful**, even when the systems still ridiculous.

CHAPTER 7
MAKING WORK SLIGHTLY LESS AWFUL

[7.1] WHEN "THIS PLACE SUCKS" ISN'T THE WHOLE STORY

By now we've covered a lot of what's wrong.

- Toxic people.
- Bad managers.
- Meetings that suck your soul out through your eyeballs.
- A system that happily eats your time and calls it "commitment."

Your inner voice spends plenty of time yelling:

"This place is a shitshow."

Which might be true.

But here's the uncomfortable bit no one really wants to hear:

You can hate the system and still have a tiny bit of space to make things less awful **for yourself** while you're in it.

You're not responsible for fixing everything. You're also not powerless.

This chapter is about the middle ground.

A lot of people resist this part because it can feel like you're letting them win. Like, "If I start making it better, am I just tolerating it?" No. You're not decorating the cage. You're making the cage less sharp while you plan your next move. There's a difference between coping strategically and pretending everything's fine.

Also, tiny improvements aren't pointless. They add up. When you reduce even one daily irritation, you free up energy you can use for things that actually matter: your health, your people, your plans, your exit strategy, your life. The workplace might still be messy, but you stop giving it every last drop of your attention like it's the main character.

- You're not "fixing the company."
- You're not spiritually ascending above it.
- You're just making your day slightly less crap so you don't feel like you're dying inside every afternoon at 3pm.

Think of it as turning the volume down on the bullshit.

[7.2] START WITH ONE QUESTION: "WHAT ACTUALLY MAKES THIS BEARABLE"

Not "what would my perfect job look like," because you'll just depress yourself.

Instead, ask:

"On the days that don't completely suck, what's different?"

Maybe it's:

- you worked with people you like
- you had some control over your schedule
- you did work that used your brain, not just your inbox
- you finished something that actually mattered

Those tiny ingredients are clues.

You might not be able to redesign your whole role, but you can try to:

- get a bit more of the good stuff
- reduce a bit of the worst stuff

This is not about being grateful for crumbs. It's about not ignoring the only levers you actually have.

[7.3] FINDING THE 20 PERCENT OF WORK THAT ISN'T TOTAL BULLSHIT

Most jobs are a mix:

- 20 percent "this is fine, maybe even enjoyable"
- 60 percent "whatever, this is work"
- 20 percent "this makes me want to close my laptop and never log back in"

If the worst 20 percent is all you can think about, it'll feel like 100 percent.

Grab a scrap of paper and split your role into three lists:

1. Things that are **weirdly okay** or even good

2. Things that are **meh but tolerable**

3. Things that **drain the life out of you**

Be honest. No one's marking this.

Then ask:

- Can I spend a bit more time on list 1?
- Can I do list 3 a little less, even by 10 percent?
- Can I move some list 3 items to list 2 with better boundaries?

Example:

- You hate presenting to senior leadership, but you don't mind mentoring juniors.
  - Maybe you offer to run a quick training for new starters and quietly avoid volunteering for big scary presentations.

- You hate random admin, but you don't mind structured reporting.
  - Maybe you help improve the reporting template once so you don't have to fight it every week.

- You hate being dragged into chaos at the last-minute, but you don't mind planning.
  - Maybe you push to be involved earlier and say no to some of the last-minute rubbish.

You're not magically turning your job into a dream. You're nudging the mix so you're not spending every hour stuck in the worst bits.

[7.4] USING "QUIET INFLUENCE" INSTEAD OF LOUD CRUSADES

Your inner voice might want to storm into a meeting and declare:

"This whole process is bullshit and we're all suffering."

You'll probably get a lovely HR-approved chat later if you do that.

Quiet influence is different. It's you asking:

"What small lever can I pull that makes this slightly less stupid without needing ten people's permission?"

Examples:

- You start sending clear agendas when **you** run meetings. People notice they suck less. Over time, others copy you.

- You share a simple checklist that makes a regular task easier. People use it because they're tired too.

- You reword a chaotic shared email template into something that makes sense and say, "Hey, I cleaned this up, want to try this version"

You're not handing in a 20-page proposal for cultural change. You're quietly improving the bits you touch.

Nobody's handing you a medal. You also don't want one. You just want less crap in your day.

[7.5] DESIGNING A "MINIMUM DECENT DAY"

Some days will be disasters no matter what you do. But you can create a rough template for what a **minimum decent day** looks like and try to hit it more often.

Ask yourself:

"If today was not great but also not soul destroying, what would it include?"

Maybe:

- one block of time where nobody's interrupting you
- one small thing finished that you can tick off
- one normal length lunch break
- one actual human moment with a coworker you like

That's it. Not "I changed the world." Just "I did enough and I'm not shattered."

Then, at the start of your day, you can quickly plan around it:

- Block out a focus slot in your calendar
- Decide which tiny thing you'll finish
- Tell yourself, "I'm taking lunch away from my screen and nobody can stop me"

You'll still get curveballs. But aiming for a minimum decent day is way kinder on your brain than aiming for "my job will suddenly be perfect today."

[7.6] BUILDING SMALL POCKETS OF CONTROL

Toxic workplaces often make you feel like you have zero control. That feeling is brutal.

You might not control:

- who runs the place
- what targets they set
- whether they're idiots

You might still control:

- how you start your day
- the order you tackle tasks
- how often you look at email
- how you respond when people dump work on you

These look small, but psychologically they're massive.

Control is basically oxygen. When you feel like you have none, your brain goes into threat mode and everything feels louder, harder, and more personal than it needs to. That's why toxic workplaces are so draining. It's not just the workload; it's the constant sense that your day belongs to other people. Reclaiming even a few tiny choices tells your nervous system, "I'm still in here. I still have a say."

Also, pockets of control work best when they're specific and repeatable. Not "be more organized," but "check email at 10, 1, and 4." Not "stop getting distracted," but "mute the channel where Kevin live-blogs his thoughts."

The smaller and more automatic it becomes, the less willpower you burn. You're building rails for your day so you don't get dragged around by every ping like a dog on a leash.

And yes, some days will still be a circus. That's fine. The goal isn't perfection, it's leverage. You're looking for tiny moves that create disproportionate relief, like closing two tabs and suddenly you can breathe again. If you can't control the idiots, at least control how often they get front-row access to your brain.

Examples of pockets of control:

- **Start the day on your terms**
  Spend the first 15 minutes planning instead of instantly diving into email.

- **Choose your hard thing**
  Do the most important or most annoying task first, then everything else feels lighter.

- **Control your inputs**
  Mute non critical channels. Check messages in batches. Unsubscribe from pointless newsletters that clutter your inbox.

- **Control how you talk to yourself**
  Swap "I'm drowning" for "this is too much and I'm doing what I can with what I've got."

You're not pretending everything's fine. You're reminding yourself you're not just a victim of the chaos.

[7.7] FINDING MICRO MEANING IN A PLACE THAT DOESN'T DESERVE YOU

Sometimes the company mission is nonsense. "Disrupting synergies to empower tomorrow" means absolutely nothing.

You don't have to buy into fake mission statements to find any meaning in your work.

Your meaning might be:

- making life easier for customers who didn't design this system either
- helping juniors avoid some of the pain you went through
- using the job to fund a life you actually care about outside the office
- getting better at skills you can take somewhere that deserves you

Ask:

"If I stop pretending the company is noble, what do I personally care about here, if anything?"

Your answer might be:

- "I like helping people solve problems."
- "I like mentoring."
- "I like making messy things clearer."
- "Honestly, I just like being good at what I do."

None of that magically fixes your workplace. But focusing on **your** reasons makes it feel less like you're suffering for nothing.

[7.8] TREATING THE JOB LIKE A STEPPING STONE, NOT A LIFE SENTENCE

When a workplace is awful, it's easy to feel trapped. Like this is it. This is your whole career now.

That feeling is heavy as hell.

Try a different frame:

"This place is my current training ground and cash machine, not my final destination."

You don't have to love it. You're using it while you quietly build an exit strategy.

That can look like:

- using awful meetings to practice facilitation skills you'll use somewhere better
- using difficult people to sharpen your conflict and boundary skills
- taking advantage of any training, courses or tools that make you more employable
- saving money when you can so you have a tiny bit more freedom later

You're not betraying your job by thinking this way. The company would absolutely move on without you if it suited them. You're just returning the favor.

[7.9] PROTECTING YOUR "AFTER WORK" LIFE LIKE IT'S SACRED

If your job feels like a trash fire, it's even more important that the rest of your life does not turn into ash with it.

You need:

- people who don't only see you as "the person from work"
- hobbies or interests that have nothing to do with your job
- small joys that remind you you're alive and not just a productivity unit

You don't have to become a wellness influencer. Just:

- go outside sometimes
- move your body in ways that don't involve walking to another meeting
- talk to someone who doesn't care about your KPIs
- have something in your week that you actually look forward to

Your job will try to colonize every part of your brain. You have to push back and say, "No, you get these hours, the rest is mine."

That might be:

- not talking about work after a certain time
- having one night a week that's "no work shit" night
- turning your phone face down and watching something stupid that makes you laugh

None of this is a luxury. It's maintenance. You cannot handle a toxic workplace if every other part of your life is empty too.

[7.10] REDEFINING "SUCCESS" SO YOU DON'T FEEL LIKE A FAILURE

Workplaces love to define success for you:

- promotion every X years
- constant hustle
- climbing some ladder that never actually ends

If you're not hitting those markers, you can easily feel like you're failing.

Try defining success for yourself instead:

- "I got through this week without sacrificing my health."
- "I didn't let one person's bad mood ruin my whole day."
- "I set three boundaries and kept them."
- "I finished work and had energy left for people I care about."

Those might not impress your CEO. They should impress **you**.

Success in a toxic workplace might simply mean:

- you didn't let it turn you into an asshole
- you didn't disappear into a numb blob
- you kept your sense of humor and some self-respect

That's not small. That's huge.

[7.11] A THREE PART "MAKE IT LESS AWFUL" PLAN

If this chapter feels like a lot, here's the simple version.

Grab a page and answer three questions:

1. **One thing I want more of in my work day is:**
   (e.g. focused time, tasks that use my brain, time with coworkers I like)

2. **One thing I want less of in my work day is:**
   (e.g. random meetings, taking on other people's work, constant interruptions)

3. **One small change I can try next week to move toward that is:**
   (e.g. block one focus slot, decline one meeting, use one new boundary phrase)

That's it. Not a five-year plan, just one small experiment.

At the end of the week, review:

- Did this make things better, worse, or neutral?
- Can I keep it, tweak it, or try a different small change?

You don't fix a toxic workplace with one dramatic move. You slowly build yourself a better experience inside it until you're ready to leave.

[7.12] IT'S OKAY TO WANT OUT AND MAKE THINGS BETTER WHILE YOU'RE HERE

You might be thinking:
"Why should I bother making this place less awful if I'm planning to leave"

Because:
- You're still here right now.
- Your brain and body are still living this reality every day.
- Small improvements now reduce the damage you carry into your next job.

Think of it like this: leaving is a plan, not a time machine. You don't get to teleport out today just because you've decided you're done. So, while you're still clocking in, you might as well stop letting the place take extra bites out of you for free. Making things better now is not loyalty. It's self-preservation.

Also, people who only "hold on until they quit" often end up crawling out of the job with their confidence shredded. They start their next role already tense, suspicious, and bracing for impact, even if the new workplace is decent. That's how one toxic job poisons the next one. Small improvements now are like disinfectant. They keep this place from becoming your entire personality.

And if anyone tries to guilt you with "If you don't like it, leave," cool. That's exactly the plan. But until that plan becomes reality, you're allowed to protect your energy, choose what you engage with, and build a daily life that isn't just work, recover, repeat. You can want out and still refuse to suffer unnecessarily on the way out.

You're allowed to:

- polish your CV
- apply for new roles
- network quietly

while also:

- saying no more often
- finding small joys
- building better daily habits

You're not betraying your future by making the present less shit.

You're just doing future you a favor by not arriving at your next job completely wrecked.

In the final chapter, we're going to zoom out and talk about the big decision your inner voice keeps circling:

"Do I stay, do I go, or do I start plotting my escape properly"

Because even if your job is still ridiculous, you deserve to feel like you have real options, not just endless screaming in your head at work.

CHAPTER 8
STAY, GO, OR PLOT YOUR ESCAPE

There comes a point where your inner voice stops screaming about individual idiots and starts asking a bigger question:

"Why am I still here"

You catch yourself browsing job sites in meetings, drafting a resignation email in your head, or saying "it's fine" while thinking "I hate this place" on loop. That loop is not you being ungrateful. It's your brain trying to protect you. When the "leave" thought keeps showing up even on a random Tuesday, that's not moodiness. That's information.

You don't need a perfect plan before you take the thought seriously. You don't have to wait until you're fully burned out, crying in the car, or hate-texting your friends at 11pm. If the idea of leaving keeps returning, treat it like a signal, not a tantrum. The point is to move from helpless to intentional, even if the first move is small.

You don't have to decide your entire future in one dramatic moment. But you do have to stop pretending you have no choice.

This chapter is about three options:

1. Stay, but on purpose.
2. Go, when it makes sense.
3. Plot your escape, quietly, while you still collect a paycheck.

Also, the moment you even hint you might leave, someone will hit you with: "The grass isn't always greener." Cool. Sometimes it isn't. Sometimes the next job is just a different flavor of nonsense. But sometimes the grass is absolutely greener, because the current lawn is on fire and full of snakes. You're not chasing perfection. You're looking for "less toxic," "more sane," or at minimum "I don't dread waking up." That's not unrealistic. That's basic self-respect.

No option is morally superior. The only "wrong" one is staying stuck and telling yourself there's nothing you can do.

[8.2] STAYING BY DEFAULT VS STAYING ON PURPOSE

Staying by default feels like this:

- "I'll just see how it goes."
- "It's bad, but I can't do anything."
- "I'm too tired to even think about job hunting."

You drift. Another year passes. Your resentment builds. Your energy drops. You wake up one day with ten years of "I meant to leave."

Staying **on purpose** looks different. You might still hate parts of your job, but you're clear on:

- why you're here
- what you're getting out of it
- how long you're willing to tolerate the current level of nonsense

For example:

- "I'm staying for the next 12 months while I pay down debt and build savings."
- "I'm using this role to get experience in X so I can move to Y next."
- "I'm staying because my manager's good, the culture's tolerable and I don't want to move right now. I'll review in six months."

Same office, same idiots, very different mindset. One feels like a prison. The other feels like a temporary arrangement.

[8.3] HONEST QUESTIONS TO ASK BEFORE YOU DECIDE ANYTHING

Before you leap or commit to staying, ask yourself some blunt questions. No fluff, no "shoulds," just reality.

1. **How bad is it really, on a scale from "annoying" to "I'm falling apart"**
   - Are you exhausted, anxious, sick, checked out
   - Or just bored and mildly irritated

2. **What's this job giving you right now**
   - Money, sure. But also, skills, connections, flexibility, decent people

3. **What's it costing you**
   - Sleep, health, relationships, mental health, dignity

4. **If you left tomorrow with a basic safety net, would you feel relief or panic**

5. **If nothing changed here for the next year, how would you feel?**
   - If your whole-body clenches at that thought, pay attention.

You don't have to write an essay. Just be brutally honest. Sometimes your inner voice has been telling you the truth for months and you've been hitting snooze.

[8.4] SIGNS IT MIGHT BE TIME TO GO

There's no perfect formula for "now you must leave," but there are some flashing lights you shouldn't ignore.

Big red flags:

1. You're regularly crying before or after work.
2. You dread Mondays so much you feel sick.
3. You're so exhausted that basic life stuff is falling apart.
4. You're being harassed, bullied or discriminated against and nothing changes when you raise it.
5. You're asked to do things that clash with your ethics and values.
6. Your body's starting to show symptoms, and your doctor's hinting work might be a major factor.

Medium red flags that add up over time:

- You've stopped caring about the quality of your work because "what's the point."
- You feel numb most days and only come alive on weekends.
- You can't remember the last time you felt proud of something you did at work.
- The only thing keeping you there is fear or guilt.

If multiple big flags are checked and you're thinking "this is me," your inner voice isn't being dramatic. It's telling you this job is doing real damage.

[8.5] WHEN IT MAKES SENSE TO STAY (FOR NOW)

On the flip side, there are situations where staying a bit longer is actually reasonable, even if the place is far from perfect.

Good reasons to stay for a while:

- You're in the middle of a time limited situation (visa, probation, maternity leave return, big life change) and you need stability.
- You're building experience in a niche that'll open much better doors soon.
- You've got a genuinely supportive manager or team that balances out wider nonsense.
- You're working toward a qualification or milestone that's easier to finish if you stay put.
- You're not in a great mental place to job hunt yet and you need to stabilize your health first.

Note the pattern: you're staying **for something**, not just because "leaving is scary."

Give yourself a timeframe:

- "I'm staying 6–12 months to get X, then I'll reassess."

Put that in your calendar. Future you will thank you when the reminder pops up and you realize you're overdue for a decision.

[8.6] HOW TO PLOT AN ESCAPE WITHOUT BLOWING YOURSELF UP

If your gut says "I need out," you don't have to slam the eject button tomorrow. You can plan a **quiet, strategic exit** while your paycheck still lands.

Think of it in three streams:

1. **Money** - so you're not trapped by panic.

2. **Skills and story** - so you're not selling "please hire me, I hate my job."

3. **Options** - so you have somewhere to land.

Money: shrink the panic

You don't need a dragon hoard. You do need a basic buffer.

That might look like:

- building a small emergency fund, even if it's just a few weeks of expenses

- cutting one or two non-essential costs temporarily so you can save faster

- not letting lifestyle creep swallow every pay rise

You're not doing a full finance overhaul. You're just giving yourself **enough** breathing room that you're not forced to say yes to the first terrible offer that comes along.

Skills and story: know what you bring

When you're fried, you forget you're good at anything. Everything feels like:

"I just answer emails and put out fires."

Grab a doc and list:

- projects you've delivered
- problems you've solved
- skills you've built (even in chaos)

Think:

- communicating with idiots under pressure
- handling stakeholders with big egos
- simplifying complex crap so normal humans can understand it
- managing competing deadlines

This is all material for your CV and future interviews. You're not just "surviving a toxic workplace." You're collecting evidence you can handle a lot and still deliver.

Options: quietly open some doors

Start small:

- Update your CV and LinkedIn, even if you never use LinkedIn much.

- Tell **one or two trusted people** you're open to opportunities.

- Browse job ads once a week to understand what's out there and what skills are in demand.

- If you're in a creative or specialized field, start a simple portfolio or list of examples.

You don't have to apply to anything yet. Just proving to yourself that other jobs exist chips away at the "I'm stuck here forever" story.

[8.7] JOB HUNTING WHILE YOU'RE STILL IN THE SHITSHOW

Looking for a job while you're working a full one is exhausting, but it's often safer than rage quitting and then scrambling.

A few survival tips:

- **Pick job search windows**
  Two evenings a week or a weekend block. Not every night, or you'll fry.

- **Use your "minimum decent day" idea**
  On heavy interview weeks, lower your expectations at your current job where you can. You're not a machine.

- **Prepare honest but safe answers**
  When they ask, "Why are you looking to move?" you don't say "because my boss is a clown and my workplace is a dumpster fire."

You say things like:
- "I'm looking for a role with more [ownership / development / stability]."
- "I've learned a lot where I am, but the culture isn't the right fit long term."

Both are true. You're not required to give them your full trauma file.

- **Watch for familiar red flags**
  If a new place says "we're like a family" or brags about "hustle culture," your inner voice should be yelling already. Believe it.

[8.8] GRIEVING THE JOB YOU THOUGHT YOU WERE GETTING

There's a weird kind of grief that comes with realizing:

- the company isn't what it pretended to be
- the manager you thought would mentor you is a mess
- the "dream role" is actually chaos in a nicer outfit

You're allowed to feel sad and angry about that. You invested time, energy, hope.

You might find yourself thinking:

- "I should've known."
- "I should've left earlier."
- "I wasted years here."

Pause.

You made the best decisions you could with the information you had **at the time**, and you didn't know it would turn out like this.

Grief is not weakness. It's you letting go of the fantasy so you can deal with the reality. Once you stop waiting for the job to become what it promised, you're free to decide what **you** want next.

[8.9] LEAVING WITHOUT BURNING EVERYTHING DOWN (UNLESS YOU REALLY NEED TO)

When you've finally decided it's time to go, your inner voice might want a big dramatic exit... "I'm going to tell them all exactly what I think and walk out."

That might feel satisfying for ten minutes. Then reality hits: references, networks, future opportunities.

If it's safe to do so, aim for a **clean, not scorched earth** exit.

The urge to go nuclear is usually your nervous system craving closure. You want them to finally admit you were right, apologize, and realize what they're losing. Spoiler: most workplaces do not deliver that movie ending. They will shrug, fill the role, and keep posting "we're hiring" like nothing happened. So, if you're fantasizing about the mic-drop speech, enjoy it privately. Then choose the exit that protects future you.

Also, remember: you can tell the truth without turning it into a live performance. If there are serious issues that need to be documented, do it calmly and in writing, and keep it factual. Dates, examples, outcomes. Not vibes, not insults. That way, if anyone tries to rewrite the story later, you've got receipts and you're not relying on someone's memory or mood.

And if references or reputation matter in your field, line them up before you leave. Identify one or two sane humans who've seen your work and will vouch for you, and quietly secure their details. You don't need the whole company to like you. You just need the right people to remember you as competent, steady, and not the person who set the place on fire on the way out.

Practical leaving steps:

- Have your next move reasonably lined up (or enough financial buffer) before you resign, if you can.

- Keep your notice period professional, not perfect. Do what's reasonable, not heroic.

- Document key handover info so the work continues, but don't work yourself into the ground trying to "prove" anything on the way out.

- If you're asked for feedback in an exit interview, be honest but measured. Focus on patterns and systems, not just roasting individuals.

Example: "Workload expectations were consistently unsustainable for the team, which led to burnout and turnover. I'd suggest looking at resourcing and priority setting."

You're not obliged to save them. You're just choosing to leave in a way that doesn't bite you later.

There are exceptions. If you've been seriously mistreated and the bridge is already a smoking ruin, you might not care about being gentle. That's your call. Just make sure you're protecting yourself legally and financially before you drop any final truth bombs.

[8.10] IF YOU DECIDE TO STAY, THIS IS WHAT THAT REALLY MEANS

If you read all this and think, "I'm staying for now," that's valid. Just don't drift. Decide.

Staying means:

- you accept this place is flawed

- you stop waiting for them to suddenly become healthy and functional

- you keep using every tool in this book to protect yourself

Create a simple "stay plan":

- Why you're staying (money, experience, specific person, life timing).

- How long you're committing to before reconsidering.

- What you'll do to make it bearable (boundaries, micro rebellions, minimum decent day).

- How you'll know it's time to re-open the "go" question.

Write it down. Otherwise, you'll wake up three years from now wondering how the hell you never left.

[8.11] YOU'RE MORE THAN THIS JOB

This feels cheesy, but it's the part your brain needs to hear most.

You're not:

- your job title
- your performance rating
- your manager's opinion
- your inbox
- your latest mistake

You're not here to live to work. You work to live. Your job is meant to help you build a life, not replace one.

You're a whole person who:

- has survived every ridiculous workday so far
- has skills and strengths you probably can't even see clearly right now
- has relationships, hobbies, history and a future that matter more than any company

If your workplace makes you feel small, broken or stupid, that says more about them than it does about you.

Your inner voice might be screaming at work. That doesn't mean it's wrong. Sometimes it's the only honest thing in the room.

You don't have to stay stuck in a toxic workplace forever. You also don't have to pull off a perfect escape plan overnight.

You just have to:

- tell yourself the truth about what's going on
- decide whether you're staying, going, or plotting
- take one small step that lines up with that decision

Then another. And another.

You don't owe any job your sanity. You don't owe any manager your soul.

You owe yourself a life where work is part of the picture, not the whole thing, and where the things you scream in your head at work are just occasional grumbles, not a constant soundtrack.

Experiment: Stop Staying by Accident

For the next 7 days, answer these three questions at the end of each workday:

- What drained me today?
- What didn't suck today?
- What would I change if I actually respected my own time?

After a week, look for patterns. If the same crap shows up every day and nothing improves, that's not "a bad week." That's your job.

EPILOGUE

YOU MADE IT.

YOUR JOB'S STILL RIDICULOUS, BUT YOU'RE LESS ALONE.

If you're reading this, you've done two impressive things.

You've survived your job long enough to want to read a book about it. And you've survived an entire book about that job without throwing it across the room.

You've seen your workplace for what it is.

You know now that:

- a lot of the nonsense is structural, not personal
- your inner voice isn't a sign you're broken; it's a sign you're awake
- plenty of other people are also smiling and saying *"sounds good"* while thinking "are you f*cking kidding me"

You've met the cast.

- The legends who keep you sane
- The walking red flags
- The bosses who help and the ones who absolutely don't
- The drama, the meetings, the inbox that never shuts up

You've picked up some things along the way:

- ways to push back without starting a war
- ways to set boundaries when everyone expects you to be always on
- ways to protect your time and energy in a place that treats both like free snacks
- ways to plan an exit that doesn't involve quitting in a blaze of glory and then panicking about how you're going to live financially

The main thing I want you to leave with is simple.

Your thoughts about your job are valid. Your job's not the full truth about you.

This workplace is one chapter, not the whole book.

If you stay for now, stay on purpose. Know why you're there, what you'll tolerate and where your line is. Use what you've read to make it **less** awful while you get whatever you need to get.

If you go, go as someone who learned from the chaos, not as someone who "couldn't hack it." There are companies held together by people like you, quietly doing more than they should in systems that don't deserve them. Taking that experience somewhere healthier isn't quitting. It's levelling up.

You were never meant to live to work. You work to live. Your job is there to fund your life, not to swallow it. Once you really believe that, a lot of the guilt you feel about setting boundaries, saying no and planning your exit starts to fall away.

So, close the book. Put it somewhere you can see the title and smirk.

Next time you're in a meeting that should've been an email, or reading an email that should never have existed, or smiling at a boss while your brain yells "are you f*cking kidding me?" remember this:

- You're not the only one thinking it.
- You're not powerless.
- You're not just your job.

You're a human being doing your best in a toxic workplace that often deserves your sarcasm a lot more than your loyalty.

And you've got a little more help now than you did before you opened this book.

ACKNOWLEDGMENTS

First, to everyone who's ever sat at their desk thinking, "Is it just me or is this completely insane?" This book is for you.

Thank you to the coworkers who keep people sane in ridiculous workplaces:

- the ones who quietly share information instead of hoarding it

- the ones who say "I've got your back" and actually mean it

- the ones who send the "that meeting was bullshit, right" message after the call

You're the reason some people make it through another week.

Thank you to the people who told me their stories, the ones they usually only share over drinks, in DMs or in whispered kitchen chats at work. The details are changed, but the spirit is the same. Your horror stories and dark humor shaped these pages.

Thank you to everyone who refused to accept "that's just how it is" as an answer, even when you stayed.

The ones who set boundaries, said no, reported problems, or walked away when the cost got too high. You're proof that work doesn't get to own you.

And finally, thank you to the readers who took a chance on a book that openly admits your job might be a shitshow. The fact you picked this up means you still believe you deserve better, even if you're not sure what that looks like yet. That belief matters. Keep it.

What Do I Do Next?

If you finished this book and thought, "Okay, I feel seen, but now what," you've got a few options.

1. **Revisit the chapters that sting the most**
   The first read gets you laughing and nodding. The second read lets you actually try the stuff. Go back to the chapters where you highlighted the hell out of things and pick one idea to test this week.

2. **Start your own "things I scream in my head at work" log**
   Not to wallow, but to notice patterns. What sets you off most: people, processes, meetings, your manager. The more you see the pattern, the easier it is to decide what to change, what to tolerate and what to leave.

3. **Share the book with someone who gets it**
   You probably know at least one other person whose brain is yelling "are you f*cking kidding me" at their job. Share the book, swap stories, use it as an excuse to talk about what you both want next.

Whatever you do after this, don't go back to pretending you're fine when you're clearly not. You don't have to fix everything overnight. Just keep doing the next small thing that protects your sanity a little more than yesterday.

ABOUT THE AUTHOR

Amelia Oliver-Lilly has survived more than one ridiculous workplace and has screamed plenty of things in her head during meetings that should've been emails.

She has worked in offices where "we're a family" meant unpaid overtime, where "quick question" meant an extra project, and where the loudest voices were not the smartest ones. Along the way she has collected stories, scripts and small acts of rebellion that made it all slightly less awful.

This is not a success manual from a perfect guru who loves every minute of corporate life. It's a book from someone who's been tired, fed up and still needed the paycheck, just like you.

If this book helped you feel a little less broken by your job, the best thank you is to tell someone else who needs to hear it too.